guide

montessori

this book was generously donated by

The Timberman Family

Allagash River Towboat

Allagash River Towboat

A Maine Logging Adventure

Story and Illustrations
by Jack Schneider

Down East Books
Camden, Maine

Cover painting copyright © 2003 by Christopher Cart
Jacket design by Dana Borremans
Interior design by Goose River Bookworks

ISBN 0-89272-601-6

Printed at Versa Press, Inc., East Peoria, IL

5   4   3   2   1

Down East Books
Camden, ME
www.downeastbooks.com
Orders: 800-685-7962
a division of Down East Enterprise,
publishers of *Down East* magazine
www.downeast.com

Library of Congress
Control Number: 2003107246

Acknowledgements

I wish to extend my appreciation to my wife Trudi, who has graciously endured my enthusiasm for this project. Also my daughter Claudia, who introduced me to the mysteries of the computer and to Ed Campbell who unscrambled my word processing endeavors. I would also like to thank Don Ludgin for his belief in this venture, and my editor, Michael Steere, who offered invaluable literary advice.

Dedicated to the Allagash Waterway and to the men who plied its forests and waters.

Prologue

In the summer of 2000, I made the hundred-mile trip by canoe from Chamberlain Lake to Allagash Village on the Canadian border. At the village, canoes are beached on Evelyn McBreide's landing. For this privilege she collects a one-dollar fee for each craft.

Evelyn is a delightful lady who fascinated me with her recollections of life in a river town in an earlier time and of her late father, Tom Pelletier, who operated the local ferry and built bateaux and towboats.

I would also like to acknowledge the contribution of Leslie Gardiner and Ransford ("Rancy") McBreide, with whom I spent a fascinating afternoon, listening to them reminisce and swap stories about working in the woods and on the towboats back in the '30s. Rancy, who is ninety-four years old at the time of this writing, has the unique distinction of having survived a ride on a boom log through nine-mile-long Chase Rapids—the wildest bit of white water on the Allagash.

Leslie and Rancy are among the last of the rugged lumbermen and rivermen who were a vital part of Maine history.

These events are but one chapter of the Maine story: A time

when four hundred ships a year sailed and steamed out of Bangor, Maine, loaded with Allagash timber destined for ports around the world.

I hope this little novel will recreate and help us better understand and treasure the history and atmosphere of that bygone era.

Jack Schneider
Georgetown, Maine

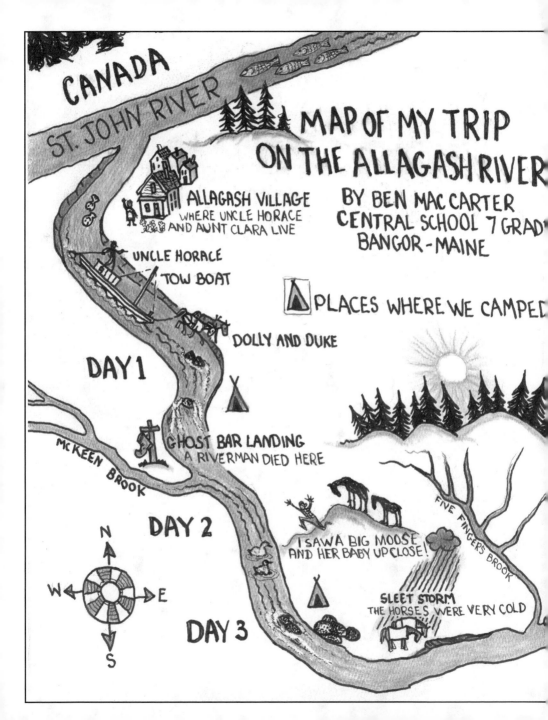

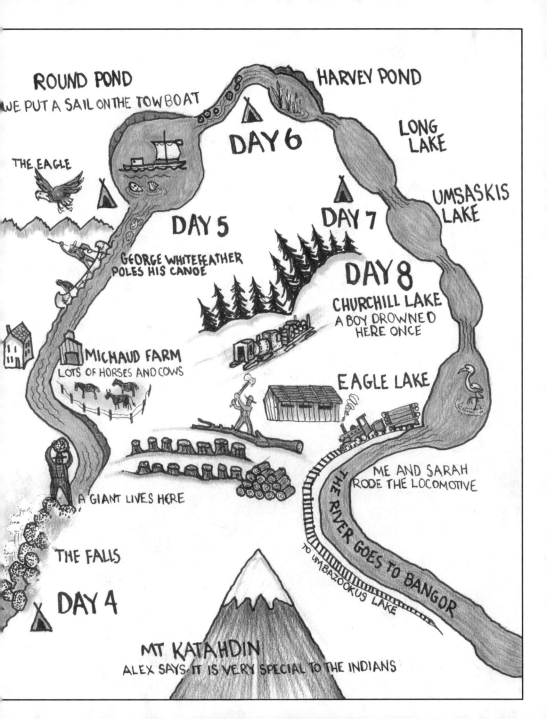

*Ben poured water into the washbowl, shivering as he splashed
a little on his face and vigorously brushed his teeth.*

November 8, 1937 — 5:30 a.m.

"Ben! Time to get up!"

Ben pulled the coverlet up around his ears and tried to ignore his Aunt Clara's sharp voice and the clatter of dishes from the kitchen. Suddenly he remembered: This was the morning his uncle was leaving to take supplies up the Allagash River to the Cousineau lumber camp at Eagle Lake, and Ben was going, too. He threw the covers back and struggled into his red and black plaid wool shirt and the corduroy knickers, which he thoroughly disliked. He longed for the day he would outgrow them and his mother would buy him long trousers at Mr. Bernard's General Merchandise and Clothing Emporium in Bangor.

Ben poured water into the washbowl, shivering as he splashed a little on his face and vigorously brushed his teeth. He stomped into his work shoes and pulled the laces extra tight. No need to take a chance losing a shoe on the fast-running river, he thought. He pounded down the loft stairs and into Aunt Clara's large kitchen, where he was surrounded by the wonderful smells of

1

Aunt Clara's kitchen was filled with the wonderful smells of baked beans simmering on the back burner of the great black woodstove and of bread and pies baking in the oven.

baked beans simmering on the back burner of the great black woodstove and of bread and pies baking in the oven. Ben pulled a chair up to the table and politely nodded "Good mornin'" to everyone, even his younger sister Sarah.

Although the sun still lay behind the eastern hills, everyone was already seated around the sturdy oak table Uncle Horace had built the year before he and Aunt Clara were married.

As he sat down, Ben noticed the marks on the edge of the table and they brought back painful memories of his ninth birthday. Ordinarily, Uncle Horace was even-tempered, but Ben had never seen him so angry as on that day. Ben had been unable to wait to test the sharpness of the jackknife he'd received and had tried the blade's keenness against the table's edge. Uncle Horace didn't actually say anything. He just quietly extended his hand for the knife. Ben spent an afternoon attempting to sand out and polish the cut marks, but he didn't see the knife again until he returned for vacation the following summer.

Aunt Clara flitted about the kitchen, filling plates as quickly as they were emptied. She set a plate with six hotcakes and a slab of country ham in front of Ben, who attacked his breakfast with enthusiasm.

Aunt Clara was a woman of ample girth, but still moved with the grace that in her youth had made her a favorite dance partner of the young men in the village. Uncle Horace had swept her off her feet forty years before. They had married and moved into the old homestead.

Uncle Horace

Uncle Horace was a fine carpenter, skillful with levers and pulleys, and had naturally turned to building and operating bateaux and towboats for use on the river. Each flat-bottomed towboat was pulled by a team of horses. The boats were sixty to seventy feet long and twelve feet wide, drawing eight to ten inches of water and, when the river had enough water, they could haul up to twelve tons of supplies.

For more than thirty years, Uncle Horace had driven his teams up the Allagash to the remote lumber camps, carrying to the woodsmen all the things they needed to survive another cutting season. However, the icy waters and backbreaking labor were beginning to take their toll. As Ben watched his uncle at his usual place next to the stove, soaking up its warmth, he wondered if this would be Uncle Horace's last trip upriver, which had been so much a part of his life for so many years.

Sarah wiggled back and forth until she had edged her chair closer to Uncle Horace. She loved her uncle with all her heart and they enjoyed teasing one another. She snuck a strip of bacon from his plate. He pretended not to notice, but when she took a second piece, he turned to her, made a face so fierce his moustache quivered, and roared in mock anger. "Sarah, some mouse is taking all my bacon!"

Sarah looked up, laughed at her uncle's pretended anger, and then frowned accusingly at him. "Uncle Horace, how come boys have all the fun? It's not fair Ben gets to go upriver and I can't! I'm going on nine and only two years younger than Ben."

A cloud of pungent smoke curled around Uncle Horace's head as he puffed on the corncob pipe that seldom left his mouth. He remained in deep thought, fingers drumming on the edge of the table, then slowly nodded in agreement. "Sarah, you're absolutely right. I tell you what we'll do. Frenchie will be coming up the river in a few days to set his traps, and I'm sure he could use an extra paddle. Can't say I approve of steel traps, but I guess a man has to do what's necessary to make a living." He avoided Aunt Clara's disapproving look and studied a fly crawling across the ceiling.

Sarah squealed with delight, bouncing up and down in her chair until Aunt Clara fixed her with a stern look and suggested she finish her breakfast.

The other four men sitting at the table, who would serve as crew on the trip, had all joined in the laughter about the disappearing bacon. Alex Murphy was the oldest. His coal-black handlebar mustache drooped over the corners of his mouth and gave him an unsmiling appearance. However, Sarah had learned Alex was a kind and gentle man and, next to her brother and her uncle, she considered him to be her best friend.

As a young man Alex had shipped out of Bangor on coastal schooners carrying ice and lumber to Boston, New York, even all the way to South America. But the woods of northern Maine eventually drew him back. Steady and reliable, Alex had worked as a lumberjack and on the horse barges for the past twenty years, most often for Horace. Over the years of working together, the two men had forged a friendship and bond of absolute trust.

Alex passed the syrup to Ezra Pease, who eyed the tall stack of flapjacks Clara had placed on his plate. He leaned back until the chair balanced on two legs and creaked dangerously under his massive weight. Ezra was ordinarily a gentle giant of a man, whose white beard gave him the appearance of a particularly jovial Santa Claus. However, over the years, several rivermen had learned, to their regret, not to push his good nature too far. A man of few words, he snapped his suspenders and paid Clara the ultimate compliment: "Clara, them flapjacks is the finest I ever et." Clara blushed with pleasure, for she was proud of her skills at the kitchen stove.

Alex Murphy

Both Ezra and Alex would serve as pike-men. Their responsibility was to keep the heavy horseboat off the boulders as they made their way south against the current. The men leapt from one gunwale to the other, continually "reading the water" and setting their steel-tipped poles.

At a nod from Uncle Horace, Jeb Harris, the third member of the crew, gulped down the last of his coffee, pushed back from the table, and unwound his six-foot-six frame from around his chair. Jeb's head nearly brushed the top of the door frame as he excused himself and left the kitchen to fetch the team from the barn. He was new to the crew, replacing George Clymer, who was considered one of the best "horseflies" on the river. The horsefly rode one of the horses along the tow-path or sometimes handled the reins while the team waded the icy, fast-flowing waters. Under George's experienced hand, teams always gave their very best. Unfortunately, George lay in the hospital at St. John, after, as Alex put it, "losing an argument with one of them almighty dangerous, new-fangled chainsaws." Jeb's handling of the team was yet to be

Ezra Pease

By tugging on the mast line, Fiddler could lift the cable over rocks and keep it from getting tangled with other obstructions in the river.

tested, and Horace could only hope he would prove to be as dependable as George.

The last member of the crew was a wiry little Irishman who went by the name of Fiddler O'Brian. Fiddler had wandered into the village some years before with little more than a violin strapped to his shoulder. He married Aunt Clara's cousin, Martha Wasgatt, had six children, and worked just enough to get by.

O'Brian's responsibility was to handle the line from the mast to the cable, properly called a halyard, which connected the team to the towboat. By tugging on the mast line, he could lift the cable over rocks and keep it from getting tangled with other obstructions in the river. Sometimes he would have to shorten the halyard by wrapping it around a belaying pin on the bow of the boat.

O'Brian had two special abilities: From a standing position he could vault over the backs of a team of horses, and he played the best country fiddle in the valley. O'Brian was in great demand at all the valley dances and always refused to accept any payment. He said his fiddling was a God-given gift and he was obliged to share it with his friends and neighbors. In view of the general shortage of cash in the O'Brian household, his wife's irritation was understandable. However, as a loyal member of St. John's Parish Church, she had to admit the difficulty in charging people for a God-given gift.

The safety of crew and team depended on the men operating like gears in a well-oiled machine. With the exception of Jeb, Uncle Horace had been up the Allagash with each of these men at one time or another and felt well satisfied with their abilities.

Uncle Horace would handle the eighteen-foot sweep oar, which steered the boat, and he would also do the cooking—an arrangement which, from past experience with Horace's culinary skills, excited no one. Clara insisted, however, that Horace's crews be well supplied for the trip up river. The victuals from her kitchen with which she provisioned the towboat were the envy of all the other towboat outfits.

Fiddler O'Brian

Horace removed the corncob pipe from the groove between his two front teeth and leaned forward. "OK, boys, I hear Jeb bringing Dolly and Duke from the barn, so we best get movin'." He slapped his leg, signaling the end of the breakfast conversation.

The jingle of harnesses and the familiar smell of the horses greeted Ben as he opened the kitchen door and stepped into the crisp November air. He watched the huge team lumber past him. Dolly and Duke each weighed more than three-quarters of a ton. Their hoofs were the size of pie plates and shod with soft-tempered shoes, which provided better traction on the slippery river rocks.

Dolly   *Duke*   *Jeb Harris*

The two horses were very much a part of Horace MacCarter's family, as other teams had been before them. Uncle Horace had a reputation for raising fine workhorses. There was always a demand for MacCarter foals and news of a newborn quickly circulated throughout the community.

Uncle Horace favored the Belgian breed for their size and power, but often crossbred to introduce the bloodlines of the smaller but tough Morgan breed. He claimed the Morgan was highly intelligent, had lots of heart, and was more nimble for working on the river.

Over the years there could be as many as three or four teams in the barn at any one time, but Horace had his favorites. Dolly was bred from one of his finest mares and a chestnut Morgan stallion owned by his brother, who lived in St. Francis. She was named after Aunt Clara's cousin Dolly, a woman of considerable size who was not particularly pleased when she learned her namesake was a very large workhorse.

Dolly was nearing twenty years of age and was a bit beyond her prime, but she still outpulled most of the competition in her weight class at the annual fairs held up and down the valley. At fair time Aunt Clara set out Uncle Horace's red bow tie and white shirt, starched so stiffly he could scarcely bend his elbows. With his straw hat pulled down at a rakish angle and white leather driving gloves, Uncle Horace always received admiring comments from the grandstand as he drove his team. "What a fine figure he cuts! So handsome in those white gloves!" and so on, Clara's lady friends gushed. Aunt Clara modestly accepted the compliments that flowed about her and made her the center of attention. Unlike many of his competitors, Uncle Horace never carried a driving whip or raised his voice while competing in pulling contests, and his teams responded by willingly throwing every ounce of energy into their collars.

In the winter, as soon as there was enough snow on the village's main street, farmers and townspeople brought out their sleighs and gathered for match races after the completion of church services. Although the rivalry was friendly, sometimes it became fierce. Occasionally a sleigh overturned and spectators scattered before the flying hoofs of a runaway. Fortunately no one had ever been seriously hurt.

Aunt Clara loved the excitement of the competition and insisted Uncle Horace bundle her in the sleigh for a headlong dash down Main Street. Dolly could still hold her own against all but the swiftest road trotters, but she never bested Doc McPherson's bay mare.

Betting was generally not approved of, but it was rumored among the ladies that the parish priest was not above placing a small wager on the side now and then—even on a Sunday.

Each year the competition gradually lessened as farmers and woodsmen began turning to tractors to work the fields and forests. Throughout the valley, trucks and automobiles were becoming a more popular form of transportation.

Duke was Dolly's last foal and had been named after Uncle Horace's favorite cartoon character in the *St. Francis Gazette*. At six years of age, Duke was still a teenager at heart and smart enough to try to get away with all he could. But he had a stern teacher. If he wasn't pulling his share of the load, or was otherwise acting up, a sharp nip from Dolly reminded him of his responsibilities.

Ben was always surprised at how nimbly Dolly and Duke, despite their great size, picked their way around rocks and stumps while hauling sixteen-foot saw logs or performing other farm chores. Uncle Horace's gaze followed the team as they moved toward the river. He spoke softly, almost to himself. "Sure going to miss handlin' the reins on what may be the last trip up the Allagash for me and Dolly and Duke. But this arthritis don't encourage me to be hoppin' in and out of the river, cold as it's gettin' to be this time of year."

Ben's breath formed little puffs in the brittle morning air as he and Uncle Horace walked to the river landing where the crew was finishing loading the supplies for the trip upriver to Eagle Lake.

The logging camps along the waterway required equipment and enormous amounts of well-prepared food to last through the winter. Originally, towboats took supplies from St. Francis up the St. John River to Allagash Village, often making the thirty-mile trip against the current in one day. From there the supplies were transferred to towboats going up the Allagash. However, in 1900 a road was built, and after that supplies were brought into the village by wagon or truck.

Lumber operations commenced in November as soon as the ground was frozen, and continued all through the winter months. By the end of January each camp would have four or five hundred thousand board feet of logs stacked in the "yards." Teams or Lombard tractors would be brought in to move the timber to the river. By March the river drives were underway and teamsters and teams left the woods before the ground thawed and became too soft for dragging logs.

Alex stood on the shore, checking the provisions as they were being loaded: "Forty bales of hay, thirty pounds of coffee, two sacks of dried beans, twelve boxes of hard crackers," Alex droned on, neatly placing a check alongside each item on the paper with a stubby pencil, which looked out of place in his large-boned, callused hand. "Thirty bags of oats, four barrels of flour, five bags of sugar, two barrels of beef jerky, one barrel of molasses, two buckets of lard, eight dozen lemons, three sets of harnesses, twelve axes, fifteen Peavey poles, six cross-cut saws, and a box of horseshoes."

Uncle Horace knew the inventory count would be accurate,

but he let his eye run over the load before signing the bill of lading. He turned to Ben and handed him the paper. "Run this over to Mr. Thomas at the store." Reaching into his pocket, he fished out a penny and flipped it to Ben. "Buy yourself a jawbreaker," he said. "But come right back. We're pushing off as soon as the horses are hitched."

By the time Ben returned, Jeb Harris was easing the team down the slippery bank. Dolly and Duke tensed their muscles, dug in their great iron-cleated hoofs and, amid flying spray, thundered into the river. In a moment they were up to their knees in the swirling water. "Back, back, whoa!" Jeb hollered. The team followed Jeb's sharp commands as he sawed and tugged on the reins, but Ben noticed that Dolly threw her head and Duke's mouth was full of foam. They did not look happy with the way the reins were being handled.

Alex and O'Brian jumped down from the barge into the cold river. They hooked the end of the cable to the horses' harness. Although the hour was early, a good number of Allagash Village's few hundred residents had wandered down to the landing to watch the castoff.

Aunt Clara came on at a dead run, skirt and petticoats flying, and balancing steaming mince

Aunt Clara came on at a dead run.

Dolly and Duke tensed their muscles . . . and, amid flying spray, thundered into the river.

and cranberry pies on the flats of her large palms. O'Brian whooped and hollered, "Can't say I'm looking forward to Horace's suppas, but I can see dessert will be DEE-licious. Clara, you sure are a doll!"

Uncle Horace frowned at O'Brian's familiarity, but there was a twinkle in his eye. "Stow it O'Brian, or that scrawny hide of yours will be feeding on canned fiddleheads for a week! We have a fair pitch of water, boys, so lets get movin' or we'll never make Ghost Landing Bar by sundown!"

With little urging, Duke and Dolly pawed at the water and threw their weight into their collars with enthusiasm. They appeared as happy as the men to be getting underway at last. The water seemed to boil around their hoofs as the team made their way to the far side of the river, struggling for footing on the slippery rocks under the fast-flowing waters. The towboat swung into the current and men and horses braced themselves for the full impact as the heavy craft reached the end of the attached line.

Uncle Horace waved his hat around his head at the spectators. The boat lurched as the cable tightened and Uncle Horace tumbled from his perch on the cabin roof. As he hit the water with a spectacular splash, everyone cheered and roared with laughter. Uncle Horace, with a chuckle at his own clumsiness, climbed back on the stern, doffed his water-soaked hat to the crowd, and tried, without success, to re-light his very damp pipe. Ben's heart beat wildly with excitement. The trip up the Allagash had begun!

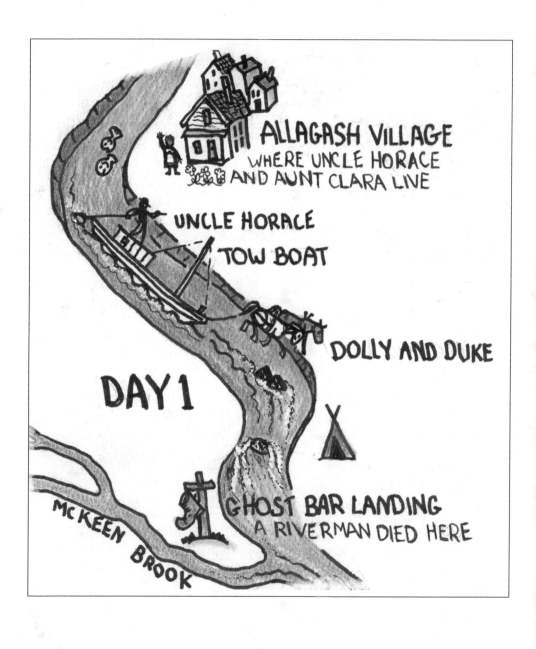

Day One

The mighty Allagash River flows northward and if a towboat goes with the current, it seems to travel nearly as fast as the wind. However, Uncle Horace's towboat was heading south, against the current, and the trip would be slow and treacherous.

There was little conversation as they negotiated the rocks half hidden beneath the surface. Occasionally, Uncle Horace issued a command to "trip the halyard" between team and towboat or one of the men called a "heads up" for a shallow spot.

Dolly and Duke ordinarily walked along a cleared path by the edge of the river, but there were many places where it was necessary for the team to wade the river and fight the swift-running current. Earlier in the season Cliff Blanchard and his sons, with their team of Clydesdales, had been hired by several of the logging companies to clear a path along the river's edge so the towboat horses could move more easily. The Blanchards had worked their way along the riverbank, removing the smaller boulders by hand and using a grappling hook pulled by their team to remove the larger ones.

"Don't seem Cliff done too good a job clearing a way for us," Ezra complained.

But Alex chided him. "Ezra, you know them ol' stones just keep rollin' back with every heavy storm, so just keep pikin' away."

Allagash Village was soon just a tiny spot in the distance, and they entered the deep quiet of the fir and spruce forest. An occasional small farm and the abandoned, overgrown ruins of homesteads carved out of the wilderness by earlier settlers slid by. Every fifteen or twenty minutes they halted to allow the team to blow and the men to rest aching muscles.

Ben sat on the cabin roof, arms clasped around his knees, squinty eyed, watching for the bear and moose Uncle Horace had promised he would see. By five o'clock they were still several miles from Ghost Bar Landing and all Ben had seen were ducks, ducks, and more ducks. Alex explained that the wood ducks and teals were gathering for the long flight south for the winter.

Dolly and Duke plodded steadily on against the current.

The sun was dropping behind the western mountains when the horse boat ground to a halt on the gravel beach at Ghost Bar.

A crude cross and a pair of rotting boots marked the spot where years before, a riverman had made a tragic misstep while breaking up a logjam and was dragged under the water. To this day, when logs block the river, it is said the anguished cries of the trapped lumberjack can still be heard. Ben knew that rivermen were superstitious, but still he was not particularly happy about camping for the night with ghosts of long ago.

Uncle Horace stepped back from the sweep-oar, stretched, and climbed down stiffly from his post. Alex and Ezra rested, leaning on their poles. Jeb dropped to the ground and rolled over on his back.

Uncle Horace glanced at him, waiting. When Jeb made no attempt to get up, Uncle Horace said softly, "Young feller, you ain't getting paid a dollar fifty a day for lazin' about. Take care of the team. First rule of the river."

Jeb glared at the older man. Uncle Horace ignored the look and continued, "You'll find the curry comb and a burlap bag to wipe the laddies down in the green tack box. Half a bucket of oats each and by the time you're finished I'll have a fine gourmet meal ready for your pleasure." Alex, Ezra, and O'Brian winced. Horace's cooking was not much valued by his crews, but few would be bold enough to tell him so. With knowing winks but little conversation the three men proceeded to set up camp. Jeb brushed down the team, muttering to himself as he set out their feed and checked for loose shoes. Uncle Horace walked away, pretending not to notice.

Ben helped unload boxes of food and cooking utensils to the beach. Ezra cut three green saplings with the axe; two forked at one end, which he pounded into the ground on each side of the fire pit. Then he placed the third sapling on the forks and hung the cast iron kettle from a rusty hook. Horace was soon preparing his "gourmet dinner" over a blazing fire.

Meanwhile, O'Brian wandered around the area picking up rusty tin cans and other trash. O'Brian sighed. "Can't understand how folks can camp in such a beautiful place and not appreciate it enough to pick up their leavin's." Uncle Horace nodded in agreement. He always insisted his campsites were cleaned up before the towboat pulled out for another day on the river. Unfortunately, many others using the river—sportsmen and rivermen alike—were not so considerate.

After a dinner of rabbit stew, beans, steaming cups of coffee, and great slabs of Aunt Clara's mince pie, the men sat around the fire drawing on their pipes and talking quietly. Ben sat huddled next to his uncle. Though he said nothing, he worried the riverman's ghost would begin calling in the night.

It took little urging for O'Brian to break out his old battered fiddle. He struck up an Irish jig and the bowing echoed off the hilltops. A great horned owl in a nearby tree hooted softly in appreciation. The men drifted into a semicircle around O'Brian, stamping their feet and clapping their hands in unison.

Suddenly Ezra, to everyone's delight, began jigging with great skill under the sparkling stars and flickering light of the campfire.

Suddenly Ezra began jigging with great skill under the sparkling stars and flickering light of the campfire.

As if in response to the flickering light and Fiddler's ever-increasing tempo, the men's shadows twisted and turned, darting in and out of the trees until they seemed to have a life of their own. After a long spell of dancing, Ezra finally collapsed on the needle-carpeted forest floor, gasping for breath, and lifted his hand in protest at Ben's urging to continue. "Ben, I'm plumb wore out. Any more, and you'll have to be handlin' my pike tomorra!"

"Ezra, how did you learn to dance like that?"

"It's called jigging, Ben, and comes from the Old Country. Learned it from m'lady. Hard to imagine a rough old coot like me married, but I was, onc't upon a time. Coal-black hair she had, and fresh from Ireland. I was just back from the war. Still in my uniform, even. Course, didn't have no whiskers then, and I weighed about fifty pounds less . . . If I say so myself, I cut a fine figure in them days."

Ben shut his eyes and found it impossible to imagine Ezra without his long, white beard and ample stomach.

"I had just got off the transport ship in St. John, and was idly walking down the street," Ezra continued, "when I saw this young lass with an armful of packages trying to open a shop door. Naturally, I went over to help. She must've thought I was some sort of a war hero, though I'd only been in France a few months when the war was over, and they'd had me cooking anyway. Some of the fellas said my food was so bad, I must be working for the Krauts.

"At any rate, me and m'lady got married shortly after and rented a nice little house outside St. Francis. We had a lovely few months together and then I told her I'd be leaving to spend the winter in the woods. My dad had always gone into the woods every fall, and I never realized how upset she'd be with my leaving. But I really didn't have much choice. I had quit school and started working as a woodsman when I was fourteen, and chopping wood was really all I knew how to do."

Ezra carefully began to braid three strands of dry brown grass together before continuing. "So make sure you get an education, Ben. Only way to make somethin' of yourself. Anyway, I come out of the woods in the spring and m'lady and me had a fine summer together. Got a few odd jobs here and there, and then come fall I had a call from Jacques Fortinier to run an operation for him way up on the St. Croix. I'd be in charge of a fifty-man crew, and me only twenty-four years old.

"M'lady begged me not to go, but the offer was too good to turn down. My crew cut a pile of lumber that winter and when I come out in the spring and went directly to our little house in St. Francis, it was empty, furniture all gone. I asked about, but no one knowed where she went. Just up and gone one day with the child. They told me she'd had a beautiful baby girl while I was up on the St. Croix. I sure wish I'd been there with her, but out in the boonies like that, wa'nt no way of knowin' what was goin' on back in St. Francis. Looked everywhere I could think for my family, and wrote several times to the only address I had over in Ireland, but never had no answer. My little girl'd be going on fifteen now, and I often wonder how and where she is."

Ezra had reached the end of the braided grass, twisted it into a necklace, and tossed it to Ben. He wore a small, sad smile. "Maybe someday she'll come lookin' for her old woodchoppin' daddy and we'll have a wonderful reunion." Ezra sighed, shifted his bulk, and turned his attention to Alex. "Now, Alex, I knowed you sailed on the coastal schooners and I'd be mighty obliged to hear more about them days."

Alex nodded. "Most pleased to Ezra. My days sailing on the coasters is going back quite a while, but I'll tell you as much as I remember."

Ben leaned forward to catch Alex's every word.

"Well, by the time I first signed on as a cabin boy in the summer of '87, the days of the sailing ships were near coming to an end, although my last voyage on a rigger was nineteen-seventeen.

"My first berth was on a pinky schooner. She was blunt nosed, broad of beam, and as slow as that molasses we was carrying from the Caribbean. Life before the mast was rugged, particularly in the winter, when ice coated every spar and shroud, but I loved every moment and can still feel that icy spray from a Nor'easter in my teeth. Got to the point when crews were hard to muster; not like earlier times when they simply got a feller drunk and before he knew it, was off on an all-expenses paid vacation for a year or two to some far-off port of call. I think the proper word for it was being 'shanghaied.' When the steamships took over the trade I figured it was time for me to come on home.

"Spent most of my years on the coasters, but did make several

26

trips to the Far East on downeasters. The downeasters took the place of the square-rigged clipper ships which was very fast, but didn't have a great deal of cargo space. I remember seeing several clippers in my early days, and they was a sight hard to forget, heeled over with every sail set and plowin' a furrow through the sea at the better part of twenty knots.

SCHOONER: A sturdy sea-going vessel with two or more masts. First built in Massachusetts, schooners were used for fishing and carrying bulk cargoes in coastal waters.

"The coasters was beamier and much slower than the clipper ships or downeasters. But they carried a heavier load of cargo, which made each run more profitable for owners and crews. The square rig worked quite well for the Orient run since the ships followed the northern tradewinds westward, then picked up the southern trade winds for the return trip; but wasn't well suited for the Caribbean run.

"I crewed on coastal schooners carryin' ice and lumber as far as South America and the Caribbean Islands. Electric refrigerators done away with the ice trade by the twenties, but it used to be a big business. The ice was cut on freshwater ponds and along the Kennebec and other rivers. They'd wait 'til the ice was about a foot thick and then saw it into blocks. 'Twas originally done by hand and mighty hard work, too, but later they used circular saws powered with a gasoline motor.

"The ice was stored up in holding sheds until it was ready to be loaded on the ships. I saw kids ride them blocks of ice down the chute running from shed to ship, and they'd flop off just before the ice dropped into the ship's hold.

"My last trip skipperin' a coastal schooner was most interesting. Left Rockland for Stonington to pick up a load of granite cobblestones bound for Trinidad, Cuba. We was just drifting into the loading wharf at Stonington when the feller on the for'ard line lost his balance and went overboard. Quick as you can say 'Johnny-jump-up', Heiner Stegmann—my first mate—jumped into that icy water and hauled the seaman out from between the ship and the dock 'fore he got crushed. Heiner was like that. A real quick thinker and mighty fine at reading the sextant, too.

"Heiner had served on sailing ships from all over the world. He was blessed with a wonderful singing voice, too, and knew sea chanteys from half a dozen different countries. He'd stand on the foredeck and bellow out them work songs while the crew was haulin' in the sails or settin' the anchor. The men would all sing at the chorus and it set up a rhythm which got everyone workin' together.

"Took two days to load all them paving blocks, and from there we sailed down to Bangor, where we took on a passel of lumber and about fifty barrels of Aroostook County potatoes. Them potatoes was packed in oak barrels called shooks. Understand these shooks were named after an Indian tribe here in Maine, though I have no idea where the tribe was located, nor how the name come to be. The potatoes were off-loaded in Cuba and the barrels filled with molasses for the return trip. Those barrels made the round trip many times over, and I suspect them County potatoes were a tad sweeter than their Canadian cousins," Alex said with a grin and a wink at Ben, "'count of that molasses."

"Next, we dropped down the coast to the little town of Phippsburg on the Kennebec where we topped off with a load of ice. Left Phippsburg on the outgoing tide and had a good run to Baltimore, Maryland, where we unloaded the ice.

"The ship was the *Molly B.* out of Bath, and as sweet a little coaster as you could imagine. Only ninety feet overall, but she could outrun any of the larger schooners. There was friendly competition between the ships, and the crews had a great deal of pleasure trying to beat each other into port. You know, Ben, every ship has its own personality and the *Molly B.* was a happy ship—as perky and frisky as any filly in your uncle's barn.

"We had fair westerlies all the way, cleared the tip of Florida and made it to Mobile, Alabama in record time. Unloaded the lumber and set sail for Trinidad with the paving blocks and a hold full of rice we picked up in Mobile.

Ben loved listening to Alex's stories and as the man spoke, Ben imagined himself sailing aboard a great ship to strange and exotic ports all over the world.

"When we made port in Trinidad, Cuba, first thing I did was take my papers to the customhouse down by the docks. Back in the early part of the century there was such lively trade between the city of Trinidad and Maine that we had our own customhouse, apart from the federal government. The customhouse was a big ol' stone building with little barred windows and a door twice the height of a man and about four inches thick. The inside was one large room for the storage of incoming and outgoing cargo. I was told the building was originally used to hold slaves as they come in from Africa, and there was still iron rings on the walls with lengths of chain which I suspect was used to tether them poor black folks while they was waitin' to be sold.

"I learned that Trinidad is one of the oldest cities in Cuba, first settled sometime in the early 1500s, and wealthy, too, from the trade in slaves and molasses and rum. Some conquistador feller named Velasques sailed up the Guarabo River and found a large village of Taino Indians. Them Indians was out in the river panning for gold, and you can imagine what happened when the Spanish saw them, since gold was what they was looking for all along. A priest tried to protect the Indians, but didn't have much luck. Within a generation—what with all the diseases the Spaniards brought, and overworking, them poor Tainos was wiped out."

Ezra pulled up a clump of dry grass and began weaving another necklace. "Alex, I'm amazed how you can remember all them names and dates and such."

Alex nodded in agreement. "Seems like yesterday. I guess I remember it all so well. But Cuba ain't like any other place I ever saw. Seemed like steppin' back in time a hundert years or more.

"In colonial times, Trinidad was a major port where folks from Africa was brought in to work the plantations. Them slaves worked six days a week, twelve to fourteen hours a day, and were treated real bad. Every so often they'd rebel against their masters, but the troops would be brought in and everything would soon be as before. In the center of town was a platform where the slaves was showed off and the buyers could see what they was purchasing. Those black fellas were supposed to be freed back in eighteen hundert and eighty-four, but they're still working today for low wages in the worst heat I've ever felt.

"As they unloaded our schooner, one fella sat there beating on a drum and singing. Nothing I understood. Probably their African language. All those stevedores would join in on the chorus, and they didn't sound none too happy. It makes me sad to think of them probably spending their entire lives loading and unloading bags of flour and sugar.

"Anyway, once the rice and paving blocks was all unloaded, bags of sugar, barrels of molasses, and I suspect, a few bottles of rum that I wasn't supposed to know nothing about came on board.

"We set sail the next evening and homeward bound with a fair wind off the port bow. We logged good time for a number of days, but then about a hundert miles off Savannah, Georgia, the fair winds died and we was becalmed. There we was, wallowing about in the swells, barely moving and mighty uncomfortable with the heat.

"Suddenly somebody shouts, 'Whale dead ahead.' We all rushed forward and were mighty surprised to see this big black thing rising out of the ocean right under our bow. Weren't no whale, but a submarine. First one any of us had ever seen, and a mighty mean looking critter she was. Had a tall tower amidships, and a hatch opened and a fellow with a hat full of gold braid popped out his head. I think he was as surprised as us. He started hollering something I couldn't understand. My first mate, Heiner, who was German, come over to the rail and the two of them started jabbering back and forth. Turned out we was at war with Germany, though it was the first any of us had heard about it.

"Heiner told me we were being told to heave to, which seemed kind of silly since we didn't have no wind and weren't going nowhere anyway. The skipper of the submarine informed Heiner he should sink us because we were enemy shipping, but Heiner must have convinced him we weren't worth the powder. Next thing I knowed their entire crew was out sunning themselves on the deck of that submarine. Several of them spoke pretty good English and wasn't long before my crew was trading cigarettes and chewing tobacco for some of the most delicious chocolate I ever et. Them fellers were quite unfamiliar with chewing tobacco, and it was most comical to see them turning various shades of green and hanging over the side.

"We spent the better part of the day tied up with that

submarine, and then along about four bells, the breeze began to freshen. I was about to cast off the lines when Heiner come up to me looking very troubled. Without him even asking I said, "Heiner if you need to go fight for your country, I understand." He never said a word. Just nodded. We shook hands and he dropped over the side onto that submarine.

"The wind filled our sails and it was quite a sight to see them Germans all standing there at attention as we moved out and picked up speed. Heiner was a fine first mate and I was surely sorry to see him go. But, you know, I got a card from Heiner postmarked Hanover, Germany several years later, but there was no return address.

"After that trip, the Coast Guard took over the *Molly B.* to use for patrolling off the Grand Banks, and so I figured it was time to come home, and I been working the river ever since."

"Alex," Ben asked, "what ever happened to the *Molly B.*?"

"Well, Ben, I was just going to skip that part of the story because it's a bit painful. I guess the Coast Guard must have put a bunch of landlubbers on her. Within a couple of months she was caught in a storm no more than fifty miles out, and all hands was lost. She was sturdy built and had lots of heart. I'm sure the *Molly B.* gave that storm quite a battle and went down fighting. But it's probably better her goin' out that way than ending her days with her bones rotting away on some tidal mud flat like the rest of the coasters."

There was silence in the camp after Alex stopped talking and

Ben's mind was racing with thoughts of slave revolts and submarines and storms at sea. Uncle Horace threw some wood onto the fire and orange sparks surged up into the dark sky.

"All you gentl'men grew up in the country," Fiddler said, and all eyes turned in his direction. "But I'm a city slicker. My folks came from the Old Country and my dad worked digging the New York subway, which was real dangerous work. They brought the Irish over at the time of the potato famine because they were willing to work for practically nothing, and if someone got hurt there was always another to take his place. Living conditions were terrible in those five-story tenements, some didn't even have indoor plumbing or running water, but it was still better than facing starvation back in the Old Country.

"I found work driving a team for a beer company in Brooklyn. I enjoyed it, but wanted to see a bit of the world. I went to see a circus out at Coney Island and got to talking to the bossman. Turns out they needed a roustabout and a hand to look after the animals, and he offered me a chance to see a bit of the world beyond the city, so I signed on.

"We headed up the Hudson River, stopping at small towns along the way. It was beautiful country and I didn't ever want to go back to the city with its terrible smells and crowds. The animals were treated well enough, considering the circus was nearly broke most of the time, and paychecks were not all that dependable.

"However, the show included a fella who signed on with his elephant. I get along just fine with most people, but he was a no-

good so-and-so who treated that poor elephant awful mean. W
we reached a new town Debbie'd be put to work raisin' the te
She wore a heavy leather harness, which went around her che
and over the shoulders, and was hooked to the top of the center
pole lying there on the ground. A hole would be dug for the butt
end, and when she put her shoulders to it, that pole went up like it
was a toothpick. That fella had a prod with a hook in the end,
which he'd jab behind Debbie's ear if she didn't move fast enough
for his liking. I told him several times I didn't think that was any
way to treat an animal, but he never listened. I think Debbie understood I was trying to help her and we had something going between the two of us. I'd scrub her back every day and take her for
a bath any time we was near a lake or pond. Debbie would roll
about in the mud and got a kick out of hosing me down and then
watching me run for cover.

"Well, one day that fella jabbed Debbie once too often with
that pole and she went a little crazy. Near took his head off and
someone went running for a gun. I begged the boss to let me try to
calm her down but nobody would listen. It took six shots 'fore she
sank to her knees. Before she took that last shot, she looked me
square in the eye, and I knowed she understood how much I cared.

I spent half that night digging a hole for a proper burial for the
old gal, then packed my duffel and left the show. I found a job driving a truck hauling supplies up to the Village, married me a
lovely woman, have a passel of kids, and I been working for
Horace on the river ever since."

r turned to Jeb. "Your turn, Jeb, and I'm sure you have

.teresting story to relate."

.ooked doubtful and searched for the right words. "After

've heard this evening, I'm afraid my life will appear most

.eresting. But first I think we should hear from Ben."

3en looked startled, but pleased that he was being included in
.e campfire talk. "Gosh, I dunno what to say. Let's see. I've lived
all my life in Bangor, but Dad says we're going to buy a little farm
so Sarah can raise sheep and I can have a team just like Dolly and
Duke. I like to play baseball, but I'm not very good, and anyway
I'd rather read books and learn about new things. That's what I
like about this trip—besides being with all of you—that I've
learned about the river, and camping out, and towboats and how
to handle a team and lots more." Ben shrugged and looked a bit
embarrassed. "Can't think of anything else to say."

The men all applauded, and Ezra nodded his head with such
enthusiasm it appeared to Ben as if his beard was dancing around
his face. "Young feller, that was as fine a speech as I've ever heard.
Keep it up, and you'll end up one of them politicians in Washing-
ton or maybe even President of these United States!" Ben felt his
cheeks burning as the men laughed good naturedly before turning
their attention back to Jeb.

Jeb thought for a long moment before beginning. "I was born
over Montreal way, and never did know my dad. He worked in a
sawmill and a shifting load of logs pinned him bad, and he died
several days later. Mother tried to support us both, but I guess it got

36

too much for her and she put me in a church orphanage when I was about four years old. We children were treated decent like, but by the time I was fourteen I'd had enough of that kind of living.

"They let me out to attend Mother's funeral and afterward I just kept going. I've been kickin' around from job to job ever since and don't have no special trade, though I think I might be good at carpentry. Eventually, I ended up in Allagash Village and Mr. MacCarter kindly hired me on, and so here I am."

"Now it's your turn, Uncle Horace." Ben shouted.

Horace slowly drew on his pipe and his voice emerged from an aromatic cloud. "Well fellers, it's been a most interesting evening. Nothing like good company and a roaring campfire to encourage one to start thinking about the past. Never really done that much with my life. I can tell you about the fine points of building a bateau or towboat or producing fine foals or a bit of the history of this beautiful river, but beyond that I'm afraid I'm pretty ignorant."

"Uncle Horace," Ben pleaded, "please tell us about building a towboat and about the river."

Horace pulled out his tobacco pouch, filled the bowl of his pipe, and firmly tamped the tobacco with his thumb. Striking a match on the leg of his pants, he lit the pipe and drew in several times until a cloud of aromatic smoke hovered over his head before he leaned back against a convenient tree trunk. "As you fellers well know, I was never much for traveling, and the Allagash has been my life for a good many years. The changing seasons, the wildlife

BATEAU:A flat-bottomed boat developed by the French rivermen in the 17th century, used on the fast flowing rivers of Canada and Maine for transporting lumber-camp supplies.

coming and going, have been enough of a world for me and I hope it stays as it is.

"Well Ben, about building a towboat. First, you need to find white oak, which is very strong, for the ribs. Each rib section is built separately and the number needed depends on the length of the boat. Usually, the ribs are spaced about six feet apart, which adds up to ten or twelve rib sections to frame up. Mind you, we build the boat upside down, and she's planked with pine or spruce. Personally, I like spruce better because it's springier and can take a heavy beating on the rocks. After stringers are run to hold the ribs in place, the planking is nailed on and cracks between the boards are caulked to make her watertight. Then the boat is flipped over, the deck and cabin attached, and she's ready for the river.

"Now, about the river itself. I had a most interesting experience oh . . . five, six years ago. A young man came knocking at the door. Seems he'd heard I was pretty knowledgeable about the Allagash and the other rivers here abouts, and asked me to sign on to guide him through the region. I

Uncle Horace began drawing a map in the dirt by the flickering light of the fire.

agreed and we loaded a bateau with enough provisions for three weeks in the woods and headed up the St. John. He had soft hands like a city feller, but by the end of three weeks on the river they was pretty well toughened up."

At this point Uncle Horace picked up a stick and, leaning forward, began to draw a map in the dirt by the flickering light of the fire.

"We continued south to Baker Pond and dropped down to Moosehead Lake. From there we headed east to Umbazooksus Lake, across the carry at Mud Pond to Chamberlain Lake and then northward down the Allagash. All together we probably traveled about three hundred and fifty miles in those three weeks."

Ben was confused. "Uncle Horace, how can we be going up the river when we're going south?"

Uncle Horace tipped back his hat, took a deep draw on his pipe and thought for a moment. "I know it's a bit confusing Ben, but let's see if we can figure it out. The Allagash actually flows north, so when we're going south, just remember we're going UP the river, and when we come back north we'll be going DOWN river. Kinda sets the world on its head. Got the picture?"

Ben nodded slowly, but still wasn't quite sure it made sense.

Uncle Horace continued. "I never saw a man so curious as that feller about everything. Always asking questions of the loggers and trappers and homesteaders we met, and writing it all down in a little book. He'd stop and watch a couple of foxes at play for hours, or some other thing that caught his fancy, until I thought we might never get back to the village. But sitting around our camp-fire at night I learned some truly amazing things.

For example, a hundred million years ago this area was nothin' but a flat plain. Apparently the earth buckled and formed the mountains. Then a million years ago everything was covered with ice which slowly melted and formed a great sea. Don't know where he got all his information, but it always sounded like he knew whereof he was talking. Said the earliest Indians arrived about ten thousand years ago and naturally used the rivers to get around. One day we was campin' on a very pleasant bend in the river. Feller said it was exactly the kind of spot the early people would have chosen for a campsite. He started grubbin' around and in no time come up with a knife-shaped piece of slate 'bout eight inches long, which I never would have noticed as being anything special. That feller said it was a skinnin' knife and thought it might be several thousand years old. It was still as sharp as a good piece of steel.

"I could go on all evening talkin' about that trip," said Horace, "but it's getting late so we best fold it in," And turning to Ben, "'Sides, this young riverman should be getting on to bed."

Ben opened his mouth to protest, but his uncle stopped him with a raised hand. "No argument Ben. We're on the river tomor-row first light, so off you go."

Ben reluctantly climbed aboard the towboat, but he found he couldn't sleep. He lay in the deepening darkness listening to the muted conversations of the men.

LOON: A bird found on north-woods lakes, usually in pairs. The loon has a haunting and tender cry which echoes across the vast lake expanses.

Finally a quiet settled over the camp and, one by one, the men climbed back on the towboat. Kicking off their heavy boots before entering the cabin, they spread out their blanket rolls and crawled in. Soon a symphony of snoring mixed with the night's sounds.

Ben was still wide awake and filled with the excitement of the day's adventures. He crawled to the cabin opening, lifted the canvas flap, and peered out. The dying coals from the fire suddenly flared, casting eerie shadows among the towering pines. Never had Ben seen the sky so high or the stars so bright, and the northern lights danced along the crest of the distant mountains, reminding him of the fireworks on the Fourth of July back home in Bangor.

The sorrowful cry of a loon drifted across the glassy, still water. Far down the river another loon answered. A massive oak reached out its arms toward Ben like a giant from a fairy tale. Shuddering, Ben pulled back into the shelter of the cabin.

He suddenly felt overwhelmed by the sights and sounds of the day and crawled carefully across the sleeping men. He curled up in his bedroll and drifted quickly to sleep.

Day Two

Ben awoke to the smells of coffee and frying fish. Jeb had risen early and found the fishing excellent. The cabin was cozy from the heat of the little cook stove and four good-sized trout sizzled in the frying pan alongside finely diced potatoes and onions, and beans.

The temperature was dropping rapidly. There was a bite to the air and a near freezing ground fog had turned every branch and twig into frosty patterns that reminded Ben of the lace curtains in Aunt Clara's sitting room.

After breakfast Ben tore a couple of pages out of the Sears and Roebuck catalog and disappeared into the bushes to use nature's outhouse, as Uncle Horace called it. He finished and walked back into the clearing just as the sun broke through the river mist. Ben could hardly believe it. Here he was—a real honest to goodness riverman! Wait until he told the kids back in Bangor!

"Come and get it, boys, or them square tails will be hopping back in the pond." Uncle Horace doled out the contents of the huge frying pan (a pan Ben learned the rivermen called a "spider"). When they were finished eating, Ezra wiped the grease from the spider with a thick slab of Aunt Clara's sourdough bread. "Sure beats washing this old thing and pollutin' the river," he declared. Breakfast over, everyone pitched in to help break camp. Food boxes and duffel were stowed away, and the stove fire thoroughly doused.

"Boys," Uncle Horace said, as he drew a map in the sand, "Here's where we are. I'd like to make it to McKeen Brook by noon. We'll rest the horses there for an hour, finish up Clara's pie 'fore it gets green around the edges, and on to McGargle's Rocks by sundown." And with that they were on their way.

The rapids were few and far between on this stretch of the river and they made good time. By eleven o'clock there were only a few more bends in the river between the towboat and McKeen Brook. Alex rested on his pike and pointed a gnarled hand toward the horses. "Look at Dolly's ears, the way they're laid back, and the way she's twitching her tail. She's telling us there are moose around."

As they rounded the next elbow in the river, Ben gasped in surprise and pleasure. This was what he had been waiting to see ever since they left the village. A huge cow moose and her yearling stood in the river, staring at the approaching craft. The moose pawed the water nervously and moved between the boat and her calf. "No use irritatin' the ol' lady, Jeb," Uncle Horace said quietly. "Take the team to the far side of the river." No urging was necessary. Dolly, in particular, had no love for the smell or sight of moose. The great creature made no move toward them as the tow-boat passed, but she continued to watch with suspicion, and then moved off into the woods.

Around the next bend, but only a short distance beyond the moose, Uncle Horace called for a lunch break. They grounded the towboat on a convenient sandbar. The horses were unhitched and wandered along the beach chomping on clumps of sweet grass. Alex had prepared jerked-beef sandwiches that morning and packed them in wooden lunchboxes. Jeb built a small fire and the crew was soon enjoying the sandwiches and cups of strong coffee, which Jeb claimed was "too thick to paddle in and too thin to plow."

"That was some almighty big moose," someone observed. Ben had a sudden desire to see the moose and her baby up close. Figuring Uncle Horace might not approve, he slipped off into the puckerbrush and climbed the knoll separating the bends in the river. He parted the brush at the top and was surpised to see the moose and calf only a few feet away.

Ben froze, amazed at the sight. He had seen moose before, but never this close up. He realized how scared he felt. Suddenly the moose sensed Ben's presence and lifted her massive head, nostrils twitching. Ben knew he shouldn't be that close, but his legs just didn't seem to work. Yet, as the moose advanced several deliberate steps toward him, Ben turned and ran. Stumbling over his own feet, he slipped and slid down the bank. The men looked up in surprise as Ben crashed through the undergrowth, shouting as he

The moose towered above them on the rise.

ran, "Moose charge! Moose charge! MOOOOOSE CHARGE!"

The moose towered above them on the rise. Uncle Horace sized up the situation. He slowly and deliberately removed the pipe from his mouth. "Time to hitch up and move on, boys." Everyone moved quietly and quickly. Ben climbed aboard the boat, his heart racing and his hands jittery from the excitement. The boat was back in the current in minutes, the moose and her baby watching as they rounded the next bend.

The only sounds for several miles were the slapping of fast-running water against the boat hull and the steady clomp, clomp of Dolly's and Duke's great hooves. As they made their way upstream, Ben sat on his perch above the deck, nervously biting his thumb. Uncle Horace was watching him. "Ben, come on astern and keep me company." The boy clambered back over the gear to where Uncle Horace squatted, resting on the sweep-oar. Uncle Horace placed his arm around Ben's shoulder. "Quite an experience you had back yonder."

Ben nodded nervously.

"Remember, Ben, every critter has his place in the woods. Ordinarily, moose and people get along just fine, but that ole lady don't figure to allow anything to endanger her youngun'. She can move faster'n Doc McPhersons's trotter and may charge when provoked. Remember, respect her space and she'll respect yours." Ben felt very much relieved when Uncle Horace slapped his leg, signaling an end to the conversation.

The rest of the day on the river was uneventful, except that

Duke lost a shoe and split a hoof slightly. Jeb replaced the shoe, all the while muttering under his breath. "Bad luck losing a shoe," he said, straightening up. He thrust his hands deep in his pockets and squinted at the sky, "Going to have heavy weather." Horace had watched Jeb replace the shoe, frowning at his superstitious nonsense, but he, too, observed the gathering clouds with concern.

They were still several miles from McGargle's Rocks when an icy sleet slanted in from the northeast. The men pulled on their greatcoats and turned up the collars. They placed blankets on the team to protect them from the sleet, and they plodded on.

There was none of the usual good-natured teasing as the crew set up camp that evening. Both horses shifted uneasily, and Duke scarcely touched his ration of feed.

Horace instructed the men to check the gear and lash tarpaulins over the cargo. Ben helped Jeb lay out hay for Duke and Dolly. The horses ignored the hay, lowered their heads instead, and turned their tails into the intensifying storm. The river ran swift and the towboat strained at its moorings.

Everyone bedded down early. Ben tossed about until someone snapped at him to be still. He slept fitfully, worrying about the horses standing out in the driving sleet, and wondering if the trees to which the boat was tied might be pulled out by their roots, leaving them all to be dashed to pieces on the rocks downstream. He fell asleep, finally, lulled by the wailing wind and the sharp drumming of a million icy fingers on the roof of the cabin. The storm continued unabated all through the night.

In the morning, Ben was awakened by the muted voices of the men. He lifted the cabin flap to a gray and miserable day. They ate a hasty breakfast, harnessed up the team, and moved out.

~~~~~~~~~~~~~~~~

Meanwhile, far to the north, the storm swirled around Allagash Village. The angry gusts grabbed the old house by its shoulders and shook until the clapboards rattled and the frame creaked and moaned in protest. But Aunt Clara's kitchen was filled with the aroma of baking bread and provided a cozy refuge against the raging storm.

Sarah snuggled up in Uncle Horace's chair by the potbellied stove and the warmth from the crackling logs felt really good on the back of her neck. Her gaze turned to the Seth Thomas clock hanging on the far wall next to the calendar with a lithographed picture of a fine yellow Packard touring car. The pendulum seemed to swing ever slower, and the monotonous tick-tock, tick-tock echoed Sarah's mood and she curled up even more tightly in Uncle Horace's chair.

"Auntie, did you always live here in Allagash Village?"

"Dear child, I've lived here all my life and have never been farther away than Bangor. Always wanted to see a bit of the world away, but Uncle has been content to keep his feet planted right here." She let out a deep sigh. "'Pears I'll never get any farther than Bangor in this lifetime.

"My people were French-Canadian. My great-grandfather came to Allagash Village from a little town outside of Quebec City. For a long time we were the only French-speaking family in this community, but I've long ago forgotten most of the French I learned as a child. The rest of the folks here and in St. Francis are all Scotts-Irish. Uncle's family came here quite a different way.

"At the time of the American Revolution there was a sizeable number of people who were loyal to the king. As I understand it, they were mostly farmers and small shop owners. The folks in favor of rebellion drove the loyalists from their homes in the colonies. Sometimes those poor loyalists were tarred and feathered and ridden out of town on a rail."

Sarah's eyes opened wide with shock and dismay. "Auntie Clara, that's awful! I can't believe people could be so cruel."

Aunt Clara nodded and smiled sadly before continuing. "The loyalists left by boat from Philadelphia, New York, and Boston and many ended up in Fredericton over at the mouth of the St. John. From there, they moved on up the river to St. Francis and Allagash Village at a time when this was just a wilderness. So, dear, that is pretty much the history of our families in a nutshell."

Sarah sat for a long time before asking the really big question on her mind. "Do you think Uncle will take me upriver next year when he totes the lumber-camp supplies?"

Aunt Clara was so long in answering that Sarah began to

think she had not been heard. Finally, Clara stopped rolling out the pie dough, laid down the rolling pin, and carefully smoothed her apron with flour-covered hands. She let out a deep sigh. "Next year is a long way off, Dear. Much can happen between now and then, but I am sure Uncle would be very pleased to have your company."

Clara felt reluctant to voice her deep concerns to the child. Horace looked tired. He had not said much, but Clara had a feeling this might be his last river trip. She brushed the flour off her apron, picked up the rolling pin, and continued rolling out the dough with more than her usual vigor.

"Sarah, why don't you go in the front room and see if Samuel has been by with the mail." Sarah knew her aunt was merely trying to find something for her to do. She was so bored! She wandered into the front room, climbed up on the bay window seat, curled herself into a ball, and stared out the rain-streaked window.

The village's one main street was usually so dusty Clara often complained that she never finished cleaning and dusting because of the dirt churned up by the huge lumber trucks and an occasional fast-moving automobile. However, the storm had turned the street into something that reminded Sarah of Aunt Clara's chocolate pudding. Pudding was one of Sarah's favorite desserts, but today the thought was not very appealing.

Above the crackling of sleet on the windowpanes there was a clanking of chain-driven wheels and the chug-chug of a powerful motor. Out of the mist emerged a massive Mack truck, slipping

*Sarah wandered into the front room, climbed on the bay window seat,
curled herself into a ball, and stared through the rain-streaked glass.*

and slithering its way through the pudding. Sarah noted with satisfaction the bulldog emblem on the hood. Jaws set and crouching forward, the bulldog seemed ready to take on the forces of nature and drive the storm away.

As the truck churned its way down the road, Sarah settled back, resigned to spending an uneventful day confined in the house. She wondered when she could get back to the important business of catching frogs along the riverbank and making her daily visit to Doctor McPherson's bay mare. The gentle animal would certainly be missing her regular carrot treat.

Sarah felt a hand pressing on her shoulder.

"I just took the loaves out of the oven. Would a slice of warm bread with strawberry jam cheer you up? And by the way, good news. Frenchie just telephoned to say he will be starting out as soon as the storm ends and the river settles down enough to be safe, probably by tomorrow morning. We've already discussed what you'll need for the trip, so go upstairs and start packing. Don't forget your heavy wool socks. Cold weather will be setting in any time now."

Sarah leapt off the window seat, bounced up and down and clapped her hands in excitement and anticipation of her adventure by canoe up the river. The wind seemed to be abating, the sleet less intense. As she raced up the stairs to begin packing for the trip, Sarah felt sure tomorrow would be a wonderful day!

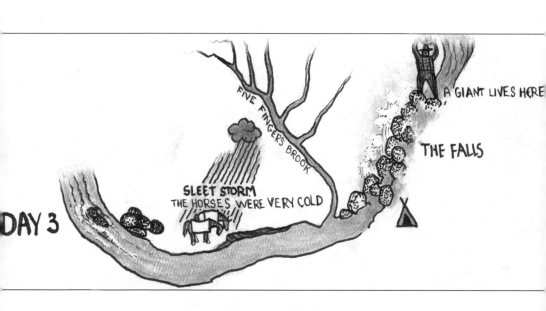

Day Three

Dolly and Duke gingerly picked their way through the rocks, moving the boat into the current. The river was rising rapidly and the animals reluctantly faced into the driving sleet. All day the crew worked in silence except for an occasional shouted warning of danger. The water was now so high that the boat, even with its twelve tons of cargo, slipped easily over rocks that only the day before would have been major obstacles. But the strong current made it heavy going for the horses. Ben sat anxiously in the cabin, peering out at the gloomy weather.

Uncle Horace stood balanced on the stern, legs widespread, pipe firmly clenched between his teeth. The sweep-oar bent dangerously under the strain. By the time they reached Five Finger Brook, the sleet had slowed to a bone-chilling drizzle, but the temperature continued to drop. The towboat stayed its course, but the last several miles to Allagash Falls were rapidly draining the last energy Dolly and Duke had to offer.

As they neared the falls landing, the boat snagged on the rocks. The water was up to the horses' bellies and they were nearly exhausted. Jeb slipped off Dolly's back.

Gaining his footing in the swirling current, Jeb grabbed the animals' bridles and pulled at their bits. Unaccustomed to such a heavy hand, the lathered horses, eyes rolling wildly, threw their heads about in confusion. "Ge' O' you lazy critters," Jeb shouted. "Move it! Move it!" He twirled the loose ends of the reins around his head and in a slashing stroke brought them down across Duke's hindquarters. Unaccustomed to the crack of leather on his flesh, Duke kicked out and became entangled in the traces. The team began to panic, floundering and pulling against one another.

Ben had never seen his uncle move so quickly. One moment he was bracing the boat against the current. The next he shouted, "Hold her fast, boys!" and leapt into the river, fighting his way through the raging waters toward Jeb. He snatched the lines from Jeb's hands and spun the younger man around by the collar. "You ever mistreat them horses again and I'll break every bone in yer sorry skinny body!" He tightened his grip and looked up at Jeb, his face purple with anger. "Give me them lines and git up there and lend Ezra a hand." Though twice the size of Horace, Jeb tripped over himself escaping the smaller man's wrath. He pulled himself onto the deck and began to tend the halyard, not meeting the other men's glances.

Under Uncle Horace's experienced and familiar hands, Dolly and Duke began to pull together. They inched forward and finally stopped, exhausted, at the base of the falls.

Ben gazed up in amazement at the thundering, cascading waters. The falls, half obscured by a sparkling, frosty mist,

He snatched the lines from Jeb's hands and spun the younger man around by the collar.

*Ben could imagine a northwoods giant standing at
the summit of the falls and hurling down boulders.*

reminded him of a great stone staircase. He could imagine a north-woods giant in the distant past standing at the summit of the falls, hurling down the boulders, which littered each step.

"I'm a bit surprised Martin Dearborn isn't already here to pick up the cargo," said Horace. "Not like him to be late, but I expect he'll be here first thing in the morning. The sun's getting low fellers, so we'll set up camp and make the carry tomorrow."

As night fell, the few remaining clouds moved off and Ben fell into a deep slumber to the soothing roar of the tumbling waters.

Day Four

he fourth day dawned clear and brilliant, but the temperature had dropped to well below freezing. Ben poked his head out of the blankets and just as quickly retreated into their warmth. "Ben, let's go, boy." Uncle Horace's words brought him back to reality. Today they would move the cargo over the falls.

He slipped into his clothes, laced up his boots, and joined the men huddled around the cabin stove. They were already downing a hearty breakfast of eggs, bacon, and the last of the cornbread swimming in amber-colored maple syrup.

Breakfast over, tin plates and coffee mugs washed, and stove fire doused, Ben and the crew rolled up their bedding before gathering on the gravel beach at the base of the falls, where a sturdy flat-bottomed wagon was drawn up well beyond the high-water mark. Uncle Horace said it belonged to Albert Spinney, a tow-boater from the neighboring town of St. John, who used the wagon to move his cargos over the carry.

The two men had grown up together, attended the same

one-room schoolhouse in the village, and handed each other a few bloody noses along the way. Albert claimed a good, fair fisticuff was the best way for boys to cement a friendship. Horace, remembering past encounters, and ruefully rubbing his jaw, allowed their friendship must be rock solid.

"Boys, Albert lets me use his wagon to move our supplies over the carry. Makes it a lot easier. Alex, you and Jeb can hitch up the horses and start moving everything to the upper landing. I'm sure Martin will be here by the time everything is moved to take the load on to Eagle Lake." Jeb dipped the frozen harness in the river water to make it more supple before hitching up Dolly and Duke. Soon, wagonload after wagonload was going up and over the carry.

Meanwhile, Ben explored along the edge of the falls, jumping from rock to rock until Ezra told him to stop. Ezra, nervous for his safety, made up a story about vicious critters, hiding in the rocks, who had chewed the legs off unwary rivermen in the past. Ben thought the story was probably untrue, but understood the message, and wandered off to look for Indian arrowheads along the river bank.

Three hours later the cargo had been moved, and Ben could see there was increasing concerns among the men as they wandered aimlessly about and waited for the towboat from Eagle Lake.

The sun was high in the sky when a canoe appeared around the river bend and ground to a halt on the beach. The tall, broad shouldered riverman who climbed out of the canoe wasted no time with formalities.

"Bad news, friends. We was badly stove up on the rocks 'bout eight miles up river. Albert says to tell you not sure how long 'for repairs can be made."

Horace gazed off at the distant mountains for a long while, puffing on his pipe, and the men waited in silence. Ben idly kicked his toe in the loose gravel of the beach. Horace, torn between responsibility for his crew and for the delivery of his cargo, was thinking how quickly the weather could turn mean this time of year. The men began to fidget in the growing silence, until Horace finally turned and addressed the group.

"'Pears to me nothing to do but take the towboat up and over the carry. Like you was sayin', Ben, nothing like learnin' to do somethin' new! Alex, you and Ezra take a couple of axes and go cut a passel of rollers to set under the keel. Meanwhile, Fiddler and me will set up a winch line."

The ring of double-bitted axes echoed across the valley, followed by the crash of falling trees, and the men were soon dragging in six-foot logs from the forest. Horace and Fiddler worked at levering up the towboat and placing the logs under the hull where they would act as rollers.

Uncle Horace turned to Ben. "I want you to go sit up on the rise. You'll have a good view from up there. Movin' the boat may be a bit tricky and I want you out of harm's way. If the cable should break, it could be wicked bad." Ben clambered up to the ridge

BLOCK AND TACKLE: A wooden block with one or more wheels for lifting or pulling heavy objects. The lifting power can be increased by adding more wheels.

overlooking both ends of the falls and found a flat rock to sit on.

"Wait until you see how slick this is going to work!" Fiddler shouted optimistically up to him. After the rollers were set, Fiddler dragged the boat cable up the slope and Horace followed with a sturdy block and tackle. Ben had noticed a large iron ring attached to a stake driven into the granite ledge at the very highest point, and wondered about its purpose. He watched the men attach block and tackle to the ring with a U-bolt and thread the cable around the block wheel.

Ben wanted to ask all kinds of questions, but he knew the men were too busy to be paying him much attention. Jeb led the team to the top of the carry, where they were hitched to the cable running from the boat up to and through the block.

At Jeb's quiet urging, the team threw their weight into their collars, the cable grew taut, and as the team moved down, the towboat slowly began to move up the grade toward the landing on the upper side of the falls.

Ben finally understood how the towboat would be moved up and over the falls.

As the team moved down, the towboat slowly began to move up the grade toward the landing on the upper side of the falls.

The men placed lines around a massive oak tree and winched
the towboat down the southern slope and back into the water.

Halfway down, the team and boat passed one another and Horace called a halt. "Need to give the laddies time to blow—and we could stand a break ourselves." The men, glad for the break, squatted down, pulled out their pipes and talked quietly. Dolly and Duke dropped their heads in exhaustion, flanks expanding and contracting like massive bellows as they sucked air in through flared nostrils.

Once the horses were breathing normally again, Horace turned to Jeb. "All right, Jeb, take it on up the rest of the way to the top of the carry."

When the towboat finally sat at the top of the carry, Uncle Horace unhitched and coiled the cable, and Ben felt proud when Fiddler called him over to help remove the block and tackle from the ring. The rest was simple. The men placed lines around a massive oak tree and winched the towboat down the southern slope and back into the water. They lost no time in reloading, and a cheer went up as the horses plunged into the pool.

The cable tightened with a snap as the boat swung back into the current once again. Above the falls the river flattened out and the going became easier. By noon they had reached Michaud Farm, a community of about twenty families. The farm was the largest operation on the upper Allagash River. It had many barns and storage sheds and was a staging area for lumber operations throughout the region. The farm supplied produce and hay, as well as livestock— cattle and swine—and the woods horses summered in its rolling pastures.

As Uncle Horace's crew sat on the rocks near the farm, finishing lunch and soaking up the sun, a canoe rounded the bend and glided silently past. Strong, graceful strokes propelled the craft on its way down the Allagash. The swarthy-skinned occupants kept their gaze straight ahead, looking neither left nor right, and Ben wondered why no greetings were exchanged.

Alex interrupted his thoughts. "See that canoe, Ben? A birch-bark canoe is gettin' to be a most unusual sight. Making one is pretty much a lost art and George there is one of the few birch-bark-canoe builders left in this part of the country. I've watched him on several occasions and it's most interesting. First, he goes out in the woods to look for white ash and birch. It's getting harder and harder to find birch trees large enough for the bark sheets he needs. He finds a flat piece of ground to build the canoe. The first thing is to pound a green ash log with a heavy board until the grain begins to separate into strips. Those'll be used for the ribs. The rib strips are stuck into the ground and bent into a series of hoops the shape of the canoe. Then these are all tied together with cordage and bark strips are laid over them. Of course, then all the ribs and bark sheets have to be sewn together, which is no mean job. Finally, pine pitch is painted on all the seams to make the canoe waterproof.

"Indians have been using canoes on the rivers and lakes as a way of gettin' around for thousands of years," Alex continued watching the canoe move slowly past. "They're light craft, easy to portage, and they track well, and stand up well, too . . . even in the white water.

"Mary, the lady in the bow of the canoe, makes beautiful little baskets from sweet grass. Some of her baskets are so small you can hardly get your finger inside, and she weaves in designs with grass dyed different colors from the juice of berries, acorns, and such. Mary says she doesn't know if the designs have any meaning, but her mama and her mama before her wove the very same designs into their baskets.

"She also weaves white and brown ash into pack baskets that are very much in demand by the locals. Mary sells some baskets in the general store down to Greenville. They're bought up by tourists from away. Don't get much for them, but says someday they are going to be very valuable. Beautiful as they are, I expect she might be right, and . . ."

"Hey, wait a minute, Alex," yelped Ben. "I'm from away, and I'd pay her lots of money for any basket I bought!"

Alex smiled, then stopped suddenly and placed his hand on Ben's arm, pointing to the sky directly above the canoe. He lowered his voice and spoke with awe. "Can you believe what we're seeing?" A bald eagle with bright white head moved majestically down the river in great, lazy circles above the canoe. They gazed in wonder as the canoe vanished around a bend, and the circling eagle became a speck in the distant sky. Alex puffed thoughtfully on his pipe. "I suspect that ol' eagle is George White Feather's

"I suspect that ol' eagle is George White Feather's totem and protector, and a sort of symbol for all the mysteries of life we don't really understand."

totem and protector, and a sort of symbol for all the mysteries of life we don't really understand."

Ben was silent for a moment, "Alex, will you tell me more about George and Mary?"

Alex leaned back on his elbow and sucked on a strand of dry grass before answering. "They are Eastern Abenaki, which means People of the Dawn. I'm afraid it's become more like People of the Sunset. Far as I know, ain't many full-blooded Indians left around here. George and his wife have probably been upriver collectin' berries and medicinal herbs.

"Before the white man came, the Abenaki were very powerful. A confederation of about a dozen tribes extended from Lake Champlain to the west, all the way to the Kennebec River in the east. For the most part they got along pretty well and it wasn't until the French and English got to fightin' that the tribes started choosin' sides and taking scalps. Matter of fact, it was the English started the practice of scalping to make sure the Indians kept an honest count of how many Frenchmen they done in.

"To the tribes, the eagle was the wings of the wind and a most powerful force. That eagle we're seein' was their Manatou or Great Spirit, but it seems like he didn't have powerful enough med'cine to protect them folks from all they's suffered through the years."

"Why didn't they speak to us?" Ben asked.

Alex chewed on the strand of grass for a long while, with a far-away look in his eye before continuing. "That's a complicated question, Ben, and I'm not sure I have the complete answer. Like I say, they's been treated quite badly through the years. Kids teased in school, and that sort of thing. Builds up from generation to generation. The distancing, you know. We all know George and Mary quite well, and strange as it might seem to you, I think choosing not to speak to us was their way of showing they still have some power over their lives."

Ben was filled with wonder. "How come you know so much about Indians?"

Alex looked at Ben's confused face. He gave Ben a chuck under the chin and ruffled his hair. "Well, Ben, I've a bit of Abenaki blood on my Mama's side and it just seems natural I should know these things."

Ben was amazed. Having a friend who's part Indian is about as good as it gets, he thought. Ben imagined him and Alex sneaking through the woods with their bows and arrows, living off the land. First thing he'd do when he got home would be to get Dad to help him make a bow and a quiver of arrows. Ben snuck another admiring glance at Alex as they finished their jerky sandwiches in silence, watching the eagle disappear behind a distant ridge of towering pines.

Uncle Horace called an end to their lunch break and they continued their slow progress. The river was still high from the torrential rains. Dolly and Duke followed the path along the river's edge but sometimes, to get around obstructions, they needed to plunge into the swift-flowing water. It took all their strength and all the skill of the crew to move against the current. Occasionally, if the horses' footing was safe, Uncle Horace let Ben ride behind Jeb on Dolly's broad back. This made him feel like he was part of the crew, and he wished he could handle the reins all by himself.

Occasionally, if the horses' footing was safe, Uncle Horace let Ben ride behind Jeb on Dolly's broad back.

Day Five

n the fifth day, as they passed through the dangerous rips above Round Pond, Uncle Horace shouted down to Ben. "Right now we're passing Turk Island. When we get to the cove, remind me to tell you what happened here."

When they tied up in the cove at the entrance to Round Pond, Uncle Horace told Ben the story. "Several years ago, Joe Jalbert was passing through here after dark. Bad idea. The water was high, with fog settling in, and they missed the crossing.

"Joe's cousin was riding on the shore-side horse. Team and rider went under. Joe's cousin was able to get the horse he was riding to shore, but Turk, a huge white horse—a favorite of Joe's—became tangled in his traces and never came up. They found him next morning several miles downriver. Joe blamed himself and named the place Turk Island in the horse's memory."

The waters were choppy. The wind had shifted back to the northwest and whitecaps were formed by the swirling gusts. Ben sat in his favorite spot on the cabin roof, looking across Round Pond, his forehead wrinkled with concentration. He figured it must be nearly as big as the Atlantic Ocean, which he had seen on the atlas back in his school room.

Uncle Horace took a long draw on his pipe. "OK, boys, load the horses and break out the oars. We got a long haul across Round Pond to Eagle Lake, so let's move out." Then, noticing Ben in deep thought, Uncle Horace turned his attention to his nephew. "'Pears to me you got something on your mind. Spit it out."

Ben hesitated and then said shyly, "Uncle Horace, remember when you carved a little boat for me and we sailed it on the village millpond? Well, why can't we make a sail from the tarpaulin and just sail down the lakes?"

There was a moment of total silence. The men looked at each other. Then Ezra placed his hands on his massive belly and roared with laughter. "I been ridin' the river for twenty years and never heard sech a wild idea before." Ezra caught his breath and then starting laughing all over again. The other men began to join in, and even Uncle Horace cracked the glimmer of a smile. Ben felt foolish for bringing up the idea and regretted saying anything.

As the laughter died down, Jeb paused from brushing Duke and cleared his throat. "Hold on there, Ezra. I ain't no riverman by profession, but there's a bit of sense in Ben's idea." He wet a forefinger and held it up to the breeze. "My finger tells me we have a following wind, which would save us from having to go around the edge of the pond or row across. It'd be much easier on the hosses." He rubbed Duke's neck and received a nicker of appreciation. Glancing in Uncle Horace's direction, he began to stroke

Duke again. As if talking to himself, Jeb spoke just loud enough for the now-attentive crew to hear: "Might want to see if it's practical at least. No harm done."

After a few minutes of discussion, the crew decided to give Ben's idea a try. Uncle Horace didn't let on, but he was secretly proud of Ben's ingenuity, whether it worked or not.

Alex unfolded the tarp and laced it onto the spare sweep oar. Jeb shinnied up the mast and lashed the oar in place. The men tied the corners of the tarp to the rails and dropped boards into the water and nailed them to the hull. Alex explained to Ben they were called leeboards and were necessary to keep the flat-bottomed craft from drifting sideways.

They then rearranged the provisions to allow space for the horses. Duke eyed the flapping canvas apprehensively, but, with a bit of coaxing, stepped onto the deck to take his place alongside Dolly. The men poled out from the shelter of the bank and the canvas sail filled with a sharp pop under the full impact of a gust of wind. The towboat creaked and groaned, then slowly began moving forward. A great shout went up from the crew. "Three cheers for Captain Ben! Hip-hip-hurray! Hip-hip-hurray! Hip-hip-hurraaaaaaaay!"

The men waved their hats and one by one reached up to shake Ben's hand. Thus was invented the first wind-powered horseboat on the Allagash Waterway. From his place on the cabin roof, Ben cupped his hands around his mouth and shouted out instructions to his crew, when to tighten or loosen the sheet lines in order to

Jeb shinnied up the mast and lashed the oar in place.

keep the sail filled. He formed a telescope with his hands and discovered far-off lands across the vast pond. Each man took his turn manning the sweep-oar—which served as their rudder—while the others lolled about on hay bales and Dolly and Duke contentedly munched their feed rations.

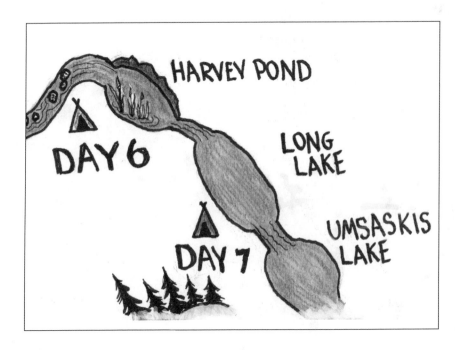

Days Six and Seven

For the next two days they sailed south over Harvey Pond and Long Lake into Umsaskis Lake (Ben noticed the terms pond and lake seemed to be used interchangeably for anything larger than a frog puddle). They passed forests yet uncut. Birds called unseen from among the dark branches. They also passed clear cuts as far as the eye could see, where nothing was left behind but litter and devastation. They rolled by an occasional farm, completely isolated except for the river, which formed the lifeblood of the valley.

For Ben it all became a blur of unfamiliar names—Croquet Brook, Squirrel Pocket, Lost Popple—and he wondered how the names had come about. Someday he would ask Uncle Horace.

From his high perch he kept a sharp lookout for the bear Uncle Horace had promised he would see. It was nearing dusk on the seventh day when Alex turned to him and whispered, "Ben, look at the set of the horses' ears. They smell something nearby." Ben could see the horses were nervous.

Suddenly, on the bluff above them, a black bear emerged from the thicket and stood watching the approaching towboat. Two small heads peeked from behind the she-bear and Ben was sure they smiled at him before being nudged back into the bushes by their mother.

Alex rested on his pike. "Bears get a bum rap. Perfectly safe. Course, if they feel cornered or need to protect their cubs, they can be dangerous. Mostly, they just want to be left alone to pick berries or maybe raid a beehive."

That night they camped on a sandbar near Churchill Depot. As they gathered around the campfire they heard a "hallo" echoing out of the darkness across the still waters. A canoe glided silently toward the shore. In the bow sat Sarah. She stowed her paddle and leapt nimbly out. Then she dragged the bow onto the beach and expertly tied a half hitch around an overhanging tree limb with the bow line.

Ben jumped up and ran over to greet Sarah, but she, spying Uncle Horace, raced across the clearing and grasped him around the legs in a bear hug, nearly knocking him over. Horace chuckled and shouted to the man in the stern of the canoe. "Quite a gilley you have there, Frenchie."

Black Bears

Sarah stowed her paddle and leapt nimbly out. Then she dragged the bow onto the beach and expertly tied a half hitch around an overhanging tree limb with the bow line.

Ben had quietly gone back to his place by the fire, alongside Ezra, who placed a comforting arm around the boy's shoulder. "Never try to understand a woman, Ben." He felt better after those words of wisdom and looked questioningly at his uncle.

"Uncle Horace, what's a gilley?" Ben asked.

"Ben, a gilley is the fellow who baits the hook, does the paddlin', and anything else the sport is either too lazy to do or is just plain incapable of doin'."

Frenchie grinned and hoisted himself out of the canoe. "I guess that makes me a sport, Horace. That young lady is one fine bowman. She can hire on anytime."

As the crew sat around the campfire, Uncle Horace told a story that made Ben and Sarah very sad. He pulled on his pipe and leaned back against the tree. "This is a sorrowful story, kids, of how Churchill Pond got its name. Some years ago two sports and their sons were campin' here on the pond. Believe the Churchill boy was about your age, Ben, twelve or so. There was some sort of boating accident. The boy drowned and they buried him over there where I'm pointing. So, remember, always be careful when you and Sarah are around the water."

Ben and Sarah looked at each other in alarm. To Ben's thinking, it seemed there was a sad story about every place they stopped.

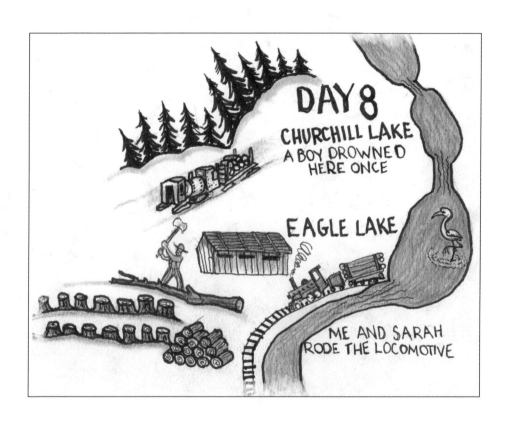

Day Eight

The next morning dawned bright and considerably warmer. They sailed across Churchill Lake and toward mid-morning entered Eagle Lake. Uncle Horace called Ben's and Sarah's attention to the far-off sound of chugging motors and men's voices: "Kids, you're soon goin' to see a sight your eyes won't believe." As they came closer, they could see a large mass of logs floating just off shore from the lumber camp.

Kids, that pile of lumber is called a boom. The booms are formed and kept together by hundreds of feet of chain running through four-foot bolts of wood called 'boom dogs.' Each boom is made up of thousands of logs that have been towed here by that steam tugboat you see anchored along the shore.

"In times past they used bateaux to haul the booms. They'd row the bateau ahead, drop an anchor in the mud, then run a line from the bateau to a raft with a capstan mounted on it. The capstan is a man-killing machine that had a line attached to the boom. The capstan would be turned by four men walkin' round and round and winding in the boom. Then the bateau is rowed ahead, the anchor reset, and those poor fellers had to bend their backs to it all over again. They'd repeat that until they'd crossed the body of water.

"The dam here at Eagle Lake controls the flow southward and from here the logs will go down the north branch of the Penobscot, all the way to Millinocket and Bangor, maybe a hundert miles downriver. They used to move booms made up of logs fifty or sixty feet in length, and I've seen old rotted pine stumps that measure five feet across. Counted the rings of one once and I figger the tree was about five hundred years old.

"Pine was the jewel of the forest. It sat in clumps along the river, which made it easy to get to for cutting, and the last stands of first growth was cut about a hundert years ago. Now spruce is just about the only log floating down the river, though no one thought very highly of 'em when there was still plenty of pine around.

"Some of that timber will be used in the Millinocket and Bangor mills and the rest shipped to who knows where. When we land, I'll show you a cable tramway three quarters of a mile long that was used to transport the logs from Eagle Lake across the

height of land to Chamberlain Lake. Amazin' clever. A sort of bucket system picked up the logs and brought them overland to the landin'. It was put in about forty years past and used 'til jest a few years ago. It was destroyed by fire several times, but they kept rebuildin' it. At peak production, half a million board feet of logs was moved in a single day. You should have seen that thing work.

"They've been usin' wood-burning locomotives between Eagle and Umbazooksus lakes rather than driving the logs. Back in '25, a mess of hundred-ton locomotives was hauled across the ice in the dead of winter using Lombard tractors. Seems they took a real chance of goin' through the ice, even though they was brought over in pieces. Now those locomotives haul six thousand cord a week, which is an awful lot of wood.

The Lombard tractors forever changed work in the woods. Developed in Maine in the early 1900s, the Lombards were steam-powered and fitted with tracks, making it possible to haul huge loads of logs over snow and mud.

"The Lombard tractors come into use about nineteen-twenty and forever changed work in the woods. One of them tractors is as powerful as twenty span of oxen, and a mite faster. The ox and horse teams can't compete. Them tractors can haul ten sledges with eighty thousand board feet in the winter over snow-covered roads. They've been working around the clock ever since. Them crews are movin' a considerable amount of wood, but are makin' a terrible mess of the forest.

"The fellows on the machines are highly skilled and make a pretty good living, but it won't last forever. In the past five or six years they hauled off most of the prime wood. Not much left now but pulpwood for the mills.

"In the old days England controlled all this area. The large pine trees was used for spars and masts on ships in the king's navy. It was a criminal offense to cut a pine with the king's stamp, and a logger would be in deep trouble. Most of the prime trees were cut long ago, but once in while you'll still find one the cutters missed.

"Today the forests is mostly owned by large companies that bought it up for pennies an acre back when the state was badly strapped. They've resisted settlement or towns growin' up on their land, which is how they keep taxes down. You'll find squatters living out there in places hard to get to. But the companies figger it's wiser to leave them folks alone rather than risk having one of 'em start an 'accidental' fire, which could destroy thousands of acres of valuable timberland."

Ben and Sarah sat alongside Uncle Horace for a long time without saying anything, gazing out across the vast expanse of Eagle Lake to the distant mountains, reflecting on the passing of the old ways and what might be expected in the future. Ben wished he could think of something to say that was as interesting as his uncle's stories.

Finally, Uncle Horace slapped his leg as if to put his thoughts behind him, and his face brightened. "Just wait till you see them locomotives!"

The horse boat worked in to the shore and the lumber-camp crew clustered about, marveling at Ben's 'sailboat.' The men wandered about, visiting with friends they had not seen in months, joshing one another, and exchanging the latest news while a bag of mail was distributed. Dolly and Duke were led up to the barn amid a chorus of welcoming neighs from the several dozen stabled woods horses.

Ezra lowered his bulk and leaned back against a convenient pine tree. "Hey kids, you want to hear what it's like to live and work in a lumber camp?"

Ben nodded eagerly, and he and Sarah sat down beside Ezra.

"Well, first off, the crews ain't becoming millionaires at a going rate of about twenty dollars a month plus room and board. There are about sixty men in this here camp, but some operations have crews of up to a hundred men. The work is real specialized; there are the cutters and toppers—a most dangerous job, the teamsters and sled tenders, the scalers who measure the logs, and the river drivers, who are called 'hogs'."

"For many years the double-bitted axe was king of the forest, and every woodsman prided himself on having an edge honed so sharp you could shave with it. Most of the felling is done now with the two man cross-cut saw, which—I admit—is faster. But I still enjoy the heft of a fine piece of steel, the thunk of the axe hittin' the tree, the chips flyin', and the crash of a great old giant comin' down.

The double-bitted axe was king of the forest.

"Now them newfangled gasoline chain-saws is beginnin' to invade the woods. They're most efficient, but so loud the noise is enough to send even the blackflies packin'.

"The cutters are separated into teams of six or eight and there can be considerable competition between the teams. They head into the woods at daybreak and work until sundown six days a week. Sunday is a time to relax, sharpen axes, and prepare equipment for the coming week.

Before the invention of the gasoline chainsaw. The two-man crosscut saw was used to cut large trees.

"It used to be most of the men working in the woods was French, with a smattering of Scotch and Irish, but now you find Swedes, Polish, and folks from places I never even heard of, all competing for scarce jobs.

"Food in most camps is pretty basic. Four meals a day. Porridge and dried apples or prunes in the morning, and for the other meals mostly beans, potatoes, and biscuits with a bit of salted meat or codfish thrown in. The two mid-day meals are prepared in the woods where the men are working, and the last meal is eaten long after dark.

"The man who runs this camp, Cousineau, has a reputation for feeding his crews well and never has a problem signing men on. But in some camps, if the cooking gets too bad, crews will pack up and leave.

"The entire crew sleeps in that bunkhouse over yonder," Ezra said, pointing out a rough-hewn log building with a cedar-shake roof. "The men line up side by side all on one long bunk and the mattress is made of pine boughs and is really quite comfortable. So, what do you think, Ben? You ready to sign on and be a lumberjack?" Ezra asked with a laugh.

Ben shook his head vigorously. "No thanks, Ezra. I think I'd rather stay a riverman."

At that moment the cook emerged from the cookhouse and gave a mighty whack with his soup ladle on the iron wheel ring hanging just outside the kitchen door. "Come and get it, boys. Sunday special and it ain't getting any better or hotter!"

The wood-slab benches groaned under the weight of men who sat to eat steaming potatoes, beans, dried codfish, cornbread muffins, and cranberry pie. It took only moments before the men

*The wood-slab benches groaned under the weight of men who sat to eat
steaming potatoes, beans, dried codfish, cornbread muffins, and cranberry pie.*

were digging into the grub. Camp rules didn't allow for jabbering while eating, so the only sounds were the clicking of knives and forks against tin plates.

When they were through with the meal, Uncle Horace rose from the table and loosened his belt several notches. "Kids, let's go over and look at the locomotive. 'Pears like Mr. Collins is stoking up for the trip with a load of logs to Umbazooksus."

"Climb on up, kids, Mr. Collins is going to take you on his next run."

Sarah found the hissing and billows of steam from the boilers frightening and she clamped her hands over her ears. Ben put his arm around her shoulder and told her not to be afraid, though he felt a bit nervous himself.

Uncle Horace, Ben, and Sarah walked over to the locomotive. Mr. Collins, the engineer, called down from the cab to Uncle Horace, who smiled broadly and nodded his head. "Climb on up, kids, Mr. Collins is going to take you on his next run." All fears forgotten, Ben and Sarah clambered aboard and the huge locomotive chugged down the tracks leading to Umbazooksus Lake. Mr. Collins instructed his young passengers how to pull the whistle cord and move the lever to control the speed.

By the time they returned three hours later, the supplies needed to last the camp over the winter had been unloaded. The towboat crew assembled and prepared to push off.

"OK, men, it's getting late," said Uncle Horace, "and I'd like to get a few miles under our belts before dark. If we leave right off, we can make camp for the night at the end of Eagle Lake. So, gentlemen," and with a wink at Sarah, "young lady, let's load the horses and head back to the Village before Clara thinks we forgot to come home for Thanksgiving dinner. Can't wait to set down at the table with that ol' gobbler and Clara's cranberries with all the fixin's. By golly, friends, you're all invited to partake!" He gave his leg a vigorous slap and they were on their way northward.

The woodsmen gathered on the shore. This would be their last contact with the outside world until the following spring. Several men waded into the icy water to help the pikemen move the flat-bottomed boat out into deeper water. Ben and Sarah stood on the cabin roof and waved to their new friend Mr. Collins until the landing was out of sight.

"I think it won't be long before this will be a ghost camp and those monsters will be just sittin' there rustin' away," Horace said softly to no one in particular as he worked the sweep oar. "Times are changing, and I'm bein' left behind. I'll take a good woods team any day. Much more intelligent than Lombard tractors and them other machines, and they don't mess up the woods so bad.

"With all the roads I hear they're plannin' on puttin' in, won't need to use the river much longer and ol' Dolly and Duke can rest their weary legs." The old man's eyes clouded over and he pulled slowly and deliberately on his pipe before continuing: "The days of the woods horse and the riverman are about over."

The now-unloaded towboat floated easily, and they had rigged Ben's sail to carry them homeward. A tranquil quiet settled over the towboat as it glided effortlessly over the mirror-like waters of Eagle Lake. The honking of geese, far off and haunting, announced the age-old race of the flocks against the gathering winter snows. A great wavering V came into view. Ben and Sarah watched the ever-changing flight pattern with fascination.

Above the honking cries and slap of wings, Ben imagined
he heard the steady beat of distant Indian drums.

To the south, Mt. Katahdin loomed over the winding river as it had for countless ages.

Above the honking cries and slap of wings, Ben imagined he heard the steady beat of distant Indian drums. One lone goose passed overhead, frantically winging to catch up with the flock from which it had somehow become separated.

Ben and Sarah sat side by side, soaking up the immensity of it all. The men lounged about, caught up in the moment. As they proceeded northward on Uncle Horace's towboat, there seemed to be a shared feeling of being alive, that moment between a time that was and a time that was to come.

Some Words From The Story

BANGOR – A major port in earlier times, which can be reached from the Allagash Waterway by traveling down the east branch of the Penobscot River. As many as 400 ships a year would sail out of Bangor carrying lumber around the world.

BEEF JERKY – Beef dried and cured so that it can be kept for long periods of time without refrigeration.

BELAYING PIN – A wood or metal pin in the rail of a boat for fastening rope.

BELGIAN HORSE – A horse originally bred to carry knights into battle and later used for farm work and hauling wagons in the cities.

BILL OF LADING – A list of cargo being shipped with a promise of delivery to the person named.

BLOCK AND TACKLE – A pulley arrangement using ropes or cable to increase lifting or pulling power.

BLOW – Allowing horses time to regain their strength after performing exhausting work.

BOW SEAT – The seat in the front of the canoe.

CARAVEL – A small and fast sailing ship used by the Spanish and Portuguese in the 16th century.

CARRY – A high point of land over which cargo and watercraft need to be transported around rapids or other obstructions.

CLAPBOARD – A wood board with one edge thicker than the other, used as siding for a house.

EMPORIUM – A store selling clothing and a variety of general merchandise.

FIDDLEHEAD – The coiled young frond of any various ferns, considered by any real Mainer to be a delicacy when boiled with salt pork.

FLAPJACKS – The term once commonly used for what we today call pancakes.

FOAL – A very young horse.

HORSEFLY – The crewmember responsible for caring for the horses and guiding them through the rock-strewn river, often on horseback.

JABBERING – Speaking quickly, usually with no particular purpose in mind.

JAWBREAKER – A hard round candy with a hot spicy flavor, which can be sucked on all day.

JOSHING – Joking and poking fun.

KNICKERS – Knee-length pants worn by young boys in earlier times.

LOFT – The area just under the roof of a house, used for sleeping and storage, or the upstairs of a barn used for the storage of hay.

MORGAN HORSE – The Morgan bloodline descends from one famous Vermont stallion named Justin Morgan. Justin once won a bet for his owner by pulling a railroad boxcar over a measured distance. The Morgan can be used as a light workhorse and a riding or carriage horse. It is noted for its loveable disposition.

NORTHERN LIGHTS – Irregular streamers of light caused by solar radiation striking the atmosphere.

PEAVEY – A heavy wood-handled tool with a metal tip and hinged hook used by lumberman to move logs.

PINKY – A small schooner for working close to shore, distinctive for its high and narrow stern.

PUCKERBRUSH – The small trees and bushes that begin to grow back after a woodlot has been severely cut over.

SHEETLINE – A rope attached to the lower corners of a sail. The sheetline is shortened or let out to make the best possible use of the wind.

STOKE UP – To feed wood into the firebox of a locomotive, heating the water and making steam to power the engine.

STOW – To pack away equipment and materials carefully.

TACKBOX – A wooden box where a horseman stores all the equipment needed to care for the horses.

TARPAULIN – A piece of canvas used to cover and protect things from moisture and the elements.

Author's Note

The Allagash Waterway is as close as we can come to a pristine river adventure here in the Northeast. Authorized as a wilderness waterway in 1966, it is under mounting pressures to make it more accessible. This magnificent heritage, originally envisioned as a sanctuary, is in danger of becoming an easily accessible play-ground, and its character may be altered or may be changed forever. For more information, Lew Dietz provides a colorful and thoughful history of the river and the region in his book, *The Allagash*.

About the Author

A professor of art and art history for many years, Jack Schneider was inspired to research this topic and write *Allagash River Tow-boat* after a canoe trip down the length of the Allagash Wilderness Waterway in northern Maine. Jack lives with his wife in George-town, Maine.